Whale Music

A Play

Anthony Minghella

Samuel French – London
New York – Sydney – Toronto – Hollywood

WHALE MUSIC

Whale Music was originally written for Eileen Ryan, Tina Perry, Jane Dale, Alison Watt, Alison Head, Audrey Middleton, and Siv Jannsen who performed the play at The Gulbenkian Centre, University of Hull, in June 1980.

The play received its first professional production in April 1981 at the Haymarket, Leicester, with the following cast:

Caroline	Michele Copsey
Stella	Carol Leader
Fran	Camille Davis
Kate	Julie Legrand
D	Sadie Hamilton
Waitress ⎫ **Veronica** ⎭	Mary Waterhouse
Sheelagh O'Brien	Anne Jameson

The play directed by Colin George

A television version was made by Granada TV the following year with Howard Baker producing and Pedr James directing. The cast was as follows:

Caroline	Leonie Mellinger
Stella	Susan Littler
Fran	Janet Rawson
Kate	Janet Dale
D	Sara Sugarman
Sheelagh O'Brien	Jean Rimmer
Veronica	Heather Williams
Waitress	Anne-Marie Gwatkin
Nurse	Judy Elrington
Staff Nurse	Sarah Livesey

CHARACTERS

Caroline
Stella
Fran
Kate
D
Sheelagh O'Brien
Veronica
Unhappy Waitress
Nurse
Staff Nurse

ACT I   Winter

ACT II   Spring

The setting is a southern coastal resort—probably the Isle of Wight

Time—the present

The setting should allow the play to move simply and fluidly from scene to scene

There are several original songs which are available for the production. Details may be obtained from Judy Daish Associates Ltd, 122 Wigmore Street, London W1H 9FE

ACT I

SCENE 1

Stella's Flat. Winter

Stella is on stage, showing Caroline the bedroom

Stella This is it. Not enormous.
Caroline (*not looking at the room much; checking the window*) No, it's fine. Do you want a deposit? I can write you a cheque.
Stella The wardrobe's full, I'm afraid. I'll clear it out tomorrow.
Caroline That's OK. I don't have much with me.
Stella I use this as a dark room in the summer. There's a blind. Great if you're into meditation.

Caroline goes to the window

Caroline The sea.
Stella Oh yeah. It's everywhere. The gulls will probably keep you awake at first. You'll get used to them. They scream at the weather.
Caroline I was born here.
Stella Oh. That makes sense. You're either born in this place or you come here to die. Listen, you couldn't manage cash, could you? A cheque's a bit . . .
Caroline Of course.
Stella Just, I don't work in the winter. I sign on as a beach photographer. But the facts of life don't interest Social Security much. They think it's my fault that nobody sunbathes in November. But they DO pay the rent and they wouldn't like it if they found out you did too. As it is I keep getting visits from unpleasant men before breakfast, demanding to examine the mattress for signs of co-habitition. Which is pretty absurd. However high in protein sperm's supposed to be, it can hardly amount to dependency. I keep telling them it would never stand up in court. They don't even manage a smile. Miserable buggers. Did you tell me your name?
Caroline It's Caroline.
Stella I'm Stella. Listen, forget the deposit—but you can give me a week's rent in advance if you like.
Caroline Thanks. Oh—is there a bathroom?
Stella Yeah. It's downstairs. If you want hot water there's a meter—10 ps—you have to kick the coinbox. (*She takes the rent*) Great. If anyone asks, I'm going to say you're an old school friend come to stay. Is that OK?
Caroline Yes, that's fine.
Stella Tremendous. (*She offers her hand*) Good to see you, old school friend.

Caroline Good to see you.
Stella Anything wrong?
Caroline No. (*Pause*) Why? (*Pause*)
Stella Hey, do you cook?
Caroline A little.
Stella A girl who cooks! I cook tins and packets. Oh—and I can thaw frozen things.
Caroline I reheat take-aways.
Stella Never touch them. I'm working hard at getting anorexia.
Caroline Why's that?
Stella Oh, it's the fashion to be unhealthy. Anyone who's anyone looks as if they could do with a good square meal. I've never lived with another girl before. When you moving in?
Caroline Now?
Stella I'll make some tea.
Caroline Uh—no thanks.
Stella Coffee? Booze?
Caroline No, I'm fine. But don't let me stop you.
Stella Is it a man?
Caroline Is what a man?
Stella Why you're here?
Caroline I didn't like the Y.W.C.A.
Stella Sorry. I know. I ask too many questions.
Caroline No. Depends what kind of reply you want. How are you?—fine— or, how are you?—falling apart, suicidal. You know—polite or honest. I'm fine on the polite.

Stella settles down with a cigarette

Stella It's cold in here. I hate the winter. I try not to go outside. The idea is to raid a supermarket in September and lock the door until April. Go in a slug; emerge a butterfly.
Caroline What do you do?
Stella Paint. No. Plan paintings. Think about them. In fact, nothing much. I mean preferably I find a man to lock in with me. Else I go maudlin. On balance I've been better off maudlin. I set one loose yesterday. There was something VERY wrong with him. He's left a smell. Did you notice? Musty. He's gone off to find a cave in Greece.
Caroline Really?
Stella My dear, welcome to 'sixty-eight revisited. This is the dregs of the beautiful people you're moving in with, you know. Record collection stops at Hendrix. South coast trying hard to be West coast. Marijuana and muesli.
Caroline You don't sound very convinced.
Stella It pales like everything else. How long do you plan to stay?
Caroline I don't know. Until the Spring.
Stella A fellow hibernator.
Caroline Oh yes.
Stella There are some things I can't work out.

Caroline Yes?

Stella Strictly polite questions. Like why not stay with parents? Where school friends?

Caroline Easy. Parents not here. Moved to Derbyshire. School friend here. Has family. I want to see her but I wouldn't want to stay. I'd trip all over the acquisitions.

Stella I see. And what—have you been at college or something?

Caroline Yes. Leeds. I'm taking a year off. That's my speciality. I took a year off before I went, too.

Stella Good?

Caroline My year off? No. Well good, yes, to have . . . to get around. That was good. The bits in between were on the whole not good. At all.

Stella Where d'you go?

Caroline Most places on the Underground. Islington the longest.

Stella Funny—you left here and went to London. With me it was the reverse. I came down here for a festival and never left.

Caroline It's the air.

Stella It's laziness. Nobody minds here. It's a lazy place. If you give up in London, half the caring agencies in the world are fighting over you. Compared to the noise those vultures make, the seagulls sound terrific.

Caroline I'm going to walk and walk and walk.

Stella Wonderful.

Caroline We used to hate tourists. Grockles, we called them. Armies of little fat red people in vests collapsing on the beach, wobbling into the water. When I think of the Summer that's all I see. Now you could shoot a gun down the high street. You can walk for hours. You can breathe a bit. I want to get my lungs full. Throw some stones.

Stella Well, don't worry about me. I won't clutter up the landscape. I'll wobble about here. You haven't got a thing about mice, have you?

Caroline No. Why?

Stella They've moved in too. I think the Greek god must have brought them with him. I went to make my toast this morning and it looked like a Polo mint.

Caroline Perhaps you'd better get a trap or something.

Stella I've got a trap. I've got two traps. I've also got poison and I'm thinking of getting an air rifle. I tell you—it's them or me.

Caroline A cat's more effective. (*She eyes Stella*) You don't like cats.

Stella At least mice just nick food. Cats expect you to buy them the stuff. I adopted a cat once. I thought it was dying or something. I'm bloody certain it gave me worms. And it stank. AND it was permanently on heat.

Caroline I thought that was supposed to be strictly OUR privilege.

Stella Yeah, well who wrote the books? Hey, are you sure you're all right?

Caroline It's nothing. I just feel a bit tired. I'll be OK in a second. Could I have some water?

Stella Sure. What about soda-water? I've got some next door.

Caroline Fine. Anything. (*She sighs*)

Caroline lies down on the bed. She suddenly retches and scrabbles for a tissue in her bag

Stella Hey, don't die on me.
Caroline I'm really sorry.
Stella Listen, have you seen a doctor?
Caroline Yes. Thanks. I feel much better.
Stella Well, what did he say?
Caroline It's a she and she said I was pregnant.

Black-out

SCENE 2

A café. Caroline is sitting at a table stirring coffee

Fran enters, "Clothkits" to the nines, carrying a couple of carrier bags

Fran (*with genuine pleasure*) Hello!

Fran and Caroline embrace

Caroline (*with genuine pleasure*) Hello!
Fran (*breathlessly*) I'm really sorry I'm late. I've had heaps to do. Absolutely mad. And I forgot to put the timer on the casserole.
Caroline Don't worry. Where's Heidi?
Fran At mum's.
Caroline What a shame. I'm dying to see her.
Fran Oh yes. She's a terror. Honestly, she's a real scream. She's crawling.
Caroline Really.
Fran You should see the house. She can destroy a room in five minutes. She tried to eat the liquidiser this morning.
Caroline Let me get you a cup of tea.
Fran Please. I'm parched. This is lovely. Five minutes peace.
Caroline Could we have two teas, please? (*To Fran*) You hungry?
Fran I'd love a scone or something.
Caroline And a scone please.
Fran Well. I got your letter.
Caroline Good.
Fran I think you're really brave. I really do.
Caroline Oh Fran.
Fran No really. I mean if Heidi had come along and I hadn't been. . . . What I mean to say is that so many girls, you know . . . just take the easy way out.
Caroline I didn't know there was an easy way out. If there had of been I would have grabbed it.
Fran No, I know. Of course. You look so well. I went all blotchy and cow-like and my hair fell out in chunks.
Caroline I feel terrible.
Fran Oh love.
Caroline I'm getting morning, afternoon and evening sickness.
Fran Ah, it'll be a girl. Have you done the needle test?
Caroline What?
Fran Dangle a needle over your lump. It works. If it goes up and down it's a

boy, and if it goes round and round in circles it's a girl. It's something to do with electricity.

A Waitress brings tea and a scone. She is not a happy waitress

Caroline Thanks.
Fran I'll get them.
Waitress You pay at the counter.

The Waitress goes

Fran I know her. You know who she is, don't you? She was in the third year when we were prefects. She was Maureen thing's friend—the one who pushed drugs.
Caroline Is it? Anyway, you do exaggerate, Fran. She told you she'd smoked a joint once.
Fran Well. Do you know who else I saw recently? Launa Carter. Vast. Like the side of a house. She was a size eight in the sixth form. Poor thing. She looked really depressed. Do you see anyone?
Caroline No. Just you.
Fran How's Miss Lawrence?
Caroline OK. Don't call her Miss Lawrence, Fran. She doesn't teach us any more.
Fran I know. But I can't think of her as Kate, somehow. It seems blasphemous.
Caroline Well don't call her Miss Lawrence when you see her. She'll have a fit.
Fran Why, is she here?
Caroline No. Not yet. But she will be.
Fran Really?
Caroline She's coming for my birthday, definitely.
Fran That will be nice. She's so fond of you, isn't she? That must have been great when she got the job in Leeds.
Caroline Yes, it was.
Fran I didn't realize you were actually sharing together.
Caroline It's Kate's house. I just have a room.
Fran It's amazing how things work out. You couldn't have guessed, could you, that you'd both end up in Leeds together?
Caroline And you a mum.
Fran Oh, come on, I was marked down as a breeder from the word go. All my brains are in my womb.
Caroline Rubbish.
Fran It's true. When Heidi appeared, something in me went click. Into overdrive. (*Pause*) I'm sorry Caroline, we're talking babies. I promised myself I wouldn't.
Caroline It's all right.
Fran No. It's thoughtless. But you get a bit obsessed. I spend so much time just looking at her. Her hands. She's so perfect. She's got Graeme's hair. Not that she's got much.
Caroline How is Graeme?

Fran Busy. He's fine. In and out like a maniac. They've made him a partner. Can you imagine? He wears a suit!

Caroline Amazing.

Fran He said to say hello.

Caroline Say hello back.

Fran Right. (*Pause*) I've brought you some things. Don't be insulted. Everything's so expensive.

Caroline Stupid. What sort of things?

Fran Here. There's a couple of sleep bras. You'll need those. And a really nice smock and trouser thing from Clothkits. The trousers have an elasticated waist so they grow with you.

Caroline You're a dear, Fran. Bless you. (*She looks in the bag. What she sees upsets her*) Thank you.

Fran I hope I'll have to ask for them back soon. (*Quietly*) Oh, Caroline. Why don't you come and stay with us? We'd love to have you. I'd be ever so useful—I'm encyclopaedic about pregnancy.

Caroline I'm not good company just now. But thanks.

Fran Think about it. It's an open invitation. It would be nice to have a grown-up around.

Caroline Grown-up! Anyway, doesn't Graeme qualify?

Fran Of course. When he's in. It's hard for men. They don't get so excited by feeds and nappies. And I believe in the family bed.

Caroline The what? No, don't tell me. Heidi sleeps with the two of you. Right?

Fran You disapprove.

Caroline Not at all. It's not my business.

Fran Graeme says it's ridiculous. But I think it'll make so much difference later on. Besides, it's marvellous. We all cuddle up and she can help herself if she gets hungry in the night.

Caroline Yes, but what about you and Graeme?

Fran What about us?

Caroline I mean, what if you want a second baby?

Fran We haven't worked that out yet.

The Waitress comes forward

Waitress We're closing.

Fran Sorry. (*She devours the scone*) Mmm. Just the job. (*Pause*) It's so nice to see you again.

Caroline Good old Fran. Constant as ever.

Fran What d'you mean?

Caroline Nothing. It's just good to see you too.

Fran I'm a twit. I almost forgot. Two special pressies. (*She produces a record*) Now, this is wonderful.

Caroline (*reading the back of the record sleeve*) Whale Music?

Fran Yes, they sing to each other. It's ever so strange. What you do is play it and relax. It's supposed to comfort the baby.

Caroline Ta.

Fran No, really. It's tremendous. It's like being very deep under water. Womb-like.

Caroline But it's already in the womb.

Fran Well, Heidi loved it. And there's simulated heart beats and things and some Purcell. Only that side's a bit scratched.

Caroline I'll play it, I promise.

Fran (*holding up a book*) And there's this. *Essential exercises for the child-bearing year.*

Caroline Oh God, Fran.

Fran They're a must, Caroline. Otherwise you'll look like a deflated balloon afterwards. And it makes such a difference for your labour. Don't make that face. It's going to happen. It's no use pretending it won't.

Caroline We'd better go.

Fran Listen, I can help with those. Graeme used to do all the counting and things for me. It's easier with someone else. We could do them at our house if you'd like.

Caroline Fran, do you think we could change the subject for a minute?

Fran Oh, sugar! I'm sorry. I know, I'm like a steamroller when I get going. That's what Graeme says. I'm sorry love. Do you want to go for a walk? You must walk a lot.

Caroline I'd like to go down to the beach.

Fran Lovely. You sit there and I'll pay this.

Caroline, alone for a second, gathers up the things. She inspects them

Fran (*to the Waitress*) How much is that then?

Waitress Fifty-five P.

Fran (*much too sweetly*) It was a lovely scone. (*To Caroline*) I wish I'd brought Heidi now. She loves sand. And you wouldn't have minded, would you?

Caroline Of course not.

Fran I thought she might have upset you.

Caroline Nobody's going to die, Fran.

Fran I know, I know. It's just I know how I'd feel.

Caroline I feel like there's glass in my guts. That's all. Everything else is just numb.

Fran Well, I'm sure a walk will do you good.

Waitress D'you think you might hurry up?

Fran I shouldn't bother with the Clearasil. It just joins the spots together.

Caroline Oh Fran!

Fran Want to hear the noise the whales make? It's like this . . . (*She makes whale noises*)

The Waitress stacks chairs on table

Waitress (*to an unseen partner*) D'you know her trouble? The husband goes up every skirt in the town . . . except hers.

Black-out

Scene 3

Stella's Flat

Caroline and Fran are doing an essential exercise for the child-bearing year. Stella is in a chair, smoking and drinking. Fran reads aloud an instruction from the manual

Stella That thing in there will be mentally disturbed by the time it drops out. It probably won't ever come out now. You can see it thinking bugger that, mate, if it's this bad in the padded cell you can forget the great outdoors.

Caroline Stella's right. This is killing me. What about my twenty minutes total relaxation, Fran?

Fran Once more.

Caroline Once more.

Fran Come on. Big effort. (*She yells out instructions*)

Stella I know what it is. It's the Karma Sutra done single-handed.

Caroline (*laughing*) I think I'm breaking something.

Fran That's good!

Stella That's good, Caroline. Break something!

Caroline Oh come on, Stella. It's great for the anorexia.

Stella So's dying. (*Getting up*) This bloody rain will drive me crazy. Who's for a drink?

Fran and Caroline loll about, exhausted

Fran I've brought some Lucozade. Do you fancy some, Caroline?

Caroline (*laughing*) I do, actually.

Stella Terrific!

Fran Your day will come. Have you got a boyfriend?

Stella Oh yeah. He's in the wardrobe right now. I keep him in kit form. No, my day won't come. I don't have Caroline's scruples.

Fran Oh, I don't know. I think you might feel different if it happened. You see—well, this is my theory anyway—it's not just a question of giving house-room to an egg for a few months . . . no, all kinds of things— hormones and what have you—are rushing about, sort of educating you for motherhood. It's very animal, I think. I mean, it's like the way your milk suddenly comes, for instance.

Caroline (*bitterly*) Where does that leave me?

Stella Right.

Fran Well, I don't know. I don't know, but it's love I'm talking about really, isn't it? I mean, I don't think that can hurt you.

Stella Oh! Come on!

Fran I think Caroline knows what I mean.

Caroline No, I don't.

Fran I wish I hadn't started this.

Stella It strikes me, Fran, you wouldn't have a problem if it came up and bit you. Well, love's great. I hear you can buy it from Habitat.

Fran I'm sorry. I don't know what you're trying to say.
Stella Yeah, well, we're on different wavelengths.
Fran I think we're probably on different planets.
Stella Welcome to Earth.

Fran looks to Caroline

Caroline Don't look at me. I lose both ways, don't I? Do you know, when I told my mother what had happened, she said, "Only a whore would sleep in two men's beds". No, not "sleep in"—"go to"—those were her words. "Only a whore would go to two men's beds." She was in the garden, pruning roses. She had a pair of those secateur things in her hand. She didn't look at me, she stared at the roses and told me it would kill my father. The strange thing is I know she didn't mean it. Basically she's kind. But those are the words that stick. Anyway, then we went indoors and everybody cried and then we had a cup of tea. From then on I've just gone from cup of tea to cup of tea. Sod the hormones, Fran.

There is a pause

Fran You haven't drunk your Lucozade.
Stella I didn't realize there were two men involved.
Caroline Oh, yes.
Stella Have you told them?
Caroline They both think the other is the father. It seemed simplest. They don't know I'm here. Just at the moment I don't think I could stomach honourable intentions.
Stella If they have any.
Fran I think you're right. Tell a man he's going to be a father and you burst a door marked hero.
Stella You're really sold on the metaphysics, aren't you?
Fran I've seen it in action.
Stella Well I don't know if it's such a good idea. Why should they get off?
Caroline I don't want to see them.
Stella Bugger seeing them. What about money? What about a bit of moral support? Why should you have to cope by yourself?
Caroline I'm not. I'm here.
Stella What kind of set-up is this? What is it when we're all clucking about like hens with our Lucozade and knitting and sticking our bloody bums in the air? Can you see a man doing that?
Fran Are you saying you think men ought to have more to do with their families? Because if that's what you mean you don't know them. Have you seen men with babies? It's laughable. I think it's a crime to leave a child with a man.
Caroline Come off it, Fran.
Stella That's just crap.
Fran Is it? I'm sorry. I wouldn't go out to work and leave Heidi with Graeme. I wouldn't trust him. They push prams—have you watched them? You'd think they were walking on nails. His idea of playing with Heidi is to sit her

in the nursery and watch her through the newspaper. That's why it's a
woman's job. Because men can't do it.

Stella You mean WON'T do it.

Fran No. It's just not in them with all the will in the world. A child goes to its
mother. You don't have to tell it.

Stella What do you expect? Your husband isn't wearing milk bottles, is he?

Fran No he isn't. And I don't think that's an accident.

Caroline You sound like you've learned it by rote, Fran. I am a woman. I
have a uterus. I bear fruit. And meanwhile, Man hunts. Drags the kill
home. Provides.

Fran Because it's always been like that doesn't make it wrong. Just
unfashionable.

Stella Just bollocks.

Caroline I don't think you believe it. But if you say it often enough you can
live with it.

Fran No! I'm sick and tired of women telling me I'm wasting my life. Envy
thy husband's penis. No. I'm sorry. You have to cut it off now, don't you?
There is something that neither of you can understand. You talk about
love, Stella—you've got no idea—because it's not love, you're right. It's
not love with men and women, it's necessity. Love is between the mother
and her child. That's why you're so poisoned. That's why men work so
hard at making everything else look more fulfilling, because it's not their
magic, it's my magic. And what's so sad, so terribly shabby, is that women
are abandoning what they have because they think men are hiding some
miracle in their hands. But there's no miracle . . .

Stella I've got to hand it to you—you can't be all bad if you hate men that
much.

Caroline (*raising her glass*) Here's to their come-uppance. Long may it last.

Fran I didn't mean to say I hated men. Is that what it sounds like?

Stella Maybe it's just your husband. I think you had him up against the wall
there—along with me and the liberated lesbians.

Caroline You didn't say lesbians.

Fran No, I didn't. And I didn't say shoot anybody either.

Stella You won't need to. If there's any truth in what you said, they'll shoot
themselves.

Fran Did you say there was a drink going? I've finished this.

Stella That's more like it, have a proper drink, that stuff will rot your teeth.

Fran I was just thinking—I was beginning to sound like a grudging hausfrau.

Stella You were—and so what? A little grudge never hurt anyone. Which is
more than can be said for hausfrauing.

Fran You get into this circle. Babies and mothers and your mothers and
baby-sitting circles and, you know, magazines and double-drainers, like—
that's a good example—do you know I was the only wife in the Close
without a double drainer and it got to me so much I couldn't get to sleep
thinking about it. But what I'm saying is, in that circle, well, no-one talks
about anything really, I mean you'd think to listen to us that nobody got
depressed or frustrated. I mean, I'm not even talking about the bloody
world, about a single bloody current event, I'm talking about our own

lives. Not a murmur. It's like it's some dreadful treachery to admit you're fed up. And then someone turns up to a coffee morning and in the middle of what's new in Mothercare says, "By the way, we're getting divorced" and bursts into tears. (*Pause*) That actually happened.

There is a pause

Caroline In Leeds nobody talks about anything BUT themselves or orgasms, or women against rape or, I don't know, Chile, and I don't see that doing much to alleviate the general misery.
Stella This is awful! God! I think I preferred the exercises. In a minute we'll all be lying on the ground wailing, which reminds me—the whale record—wow!
Fran Oh, do you like it?
Stella No, it's absolutely horrendous, but it's got rid of the mice!
Caroline Stella rigged up the stereo in the kitchen.
Stella They ran up the street waving white flags.
Fran It's not that bad.

Stella imitates whale music

Caroline I'd like to go out.
Stella It's raining.
Caroline I don't mean the beach. I mean US go out.
Fran Where?
Caroline I don't know. What about a disco?
Stella You want to go dancing.
Caroline I do. Come on, Fran, we could take the exercises.
Fran I haven't been to a disco since, oh I don't know. Can't remember.
Caroline Right. Where do we go? You're the expert Stella.
Stella At this time of year? There might be a late funeral.
Caroline Boring. So where were you on Saturday?
Stella The Sixty-nine.
Caroline What's wrong with that?
Stella We can't go there. It's really nasty. Besides, it's not a disco, it's a cattle market.
Caroline We could ignore all that and just have a dance.
Stella Around our bags?
Fran I can't. I ought to get back.
Caroline I thought Heidi was sleeping at your mum's.
Fran No, but Graeme will be there. The football club always go for a drink after training.
Caroline Great. You can dance with Graeme.
Stella And we'll have the football club.
Caroline That's settled then.
Fran What if he's dancing with someone else?
Stella I would think it's pretty unlikely he WON'T be dancing with someone else.
Fran I know.
Stella Well, look love, I've never met your husband but it strikes me it

wouldn't hurt to remind him that you can wiggle your udders with the best
of them.

Fran You're right. You've never met him.

Caroline Well, OK, let's go somewhere else.

Fran No. We'll go there. Sod him. Can I borrow something to wear?

Stella A holster?

Fran Hmm. It's dangerous, isn't it? Talk—I mean, women talking. If we ever
had a union the world would stop dead.

Stella Well, it certainly puts a whole new light on withdrawing labour.

Caroline groans

Fran I'm enjoying this. I'm really enjoying myself.

Black-out

SCENE 4

Stella's Flat. Morning

*Caroline is alone, going through a bundle of letters and a parcel. She is wearing
a dressing gown*

Stella enters, dressed as the previous scene but rather the worse for wear

Stella Oh, you're up.

Caroline D'you want coffee?

Stella No.

Caroline makes a point of going through the letters

OK, I know what you're thinking.

Caroline Do you?

Stella Look, have you got any money?

Caroline Yes.

Stella I need a cigarette and a shower.

Caroline I'll get my purse.

Stella We can take it off the rent.

Caroline I've paid the rent.

Caroline exits for her purse and returns immediately

Stella Next week's then. How did you get home?

Caroline I walked.

Stella What happened to Fran?

Caroline They left. I didn't hear what was said. But the headlines were plain
enough.

Stella Not good.

Caroline No.

Stella Well, it's her own fault. What did she expect?

Caroline It's our fault. We should have gone somewhere else. We shouldn't
have gone at all.

Stella That why you didn't stay?

Caroline I was by myself.

Stella Not when I started dancing.

Caroline Oh no, not then—then I was being massaged by a psychopath.

Stella I thought that's what you went for.

Caroline I thought I was going out with you and Fran. Anyway, let's forget it. (*Pointedly*) How was YOUR night?

Stella Oh, piss off.

Caroline (*looking in her purse*) Will a pound do, Stella? (*Pause. Then, thawing*) You don't have to feel guilty.

Stella No, I don't have to. Do you feel OK?

Caroline (*smiling*) Awful.

Stella (*smiling*) Me too.

Caroline (*pointing to the parcel*) From my mother. Red Cross parcel. I've just eaten a pound bar of fruit and nut. I saved you a piece.

Stella (*accepting it and sitting down*) I don't know why I did it. Reflex. Didn't even fancy him. D'you know what he does? You won't believe this—he works for Social Security.

Caroline (*laughing*) Was he on duty?

Stella He was barely conscious. Stupid, isn't it? But it was raining and he had a car, and I didn't fancy walking home much. And then, of course, this morning it's still raining and I had even further to walk. (*She sighs*) I must have a shower. (*Looking at the pile of letters and the parcel*) Someone's popular.

Caroline Stella. Graeme. . . .

Stella What about him?

Caroline You know him don't you?

Stella Yes, probably. It's a small place. I know everyone.

Caroline That's not what I meant. I don't think it was reflex that made you go off so suddenly.

Stella (*sighing*) I know him.

Caroline I knew it—what a joke.

Stella I didn't find it funny.

Caroline You've slept with him. Right?

Stella Yes, I've slept with him.

Caroline So've I. So have I. (*She pauses*) That's pretty funny, isn't it?

Stella It's pretty sick.

Caroline Oh yes.

Stella When?

Caroline He was the first. When we were at school.

Stella Oh. (*Meaning* "*Oh, before Fran*")

Caroline No—not before Fran. They were already going out. I'll spare you the details.

Stella Drunk?

Caroline It wasn't just once. Most of the summer. I'm not proud of it.

Stella Does Fran know?

Caroline No.

Stella Well, you live and learn.

Caroline You certainly do.

Stella Has he changed much?

Caroline Look it was a farce—the whole thing. Sordid. Passionless. Thumping of bones.

Stella I just can't see it. You.

Caroline It has happened. (*Referring to her stomach*) Very much so.

Stella Means nothing to me. When I see a pregnant woman, sex seems a million miles away.

Caroline I'm afraid there were no angels.

Stella Can I feel?

Stella gets up and puts her hand on Caroline's stomach

Stella Amazing. It's always amazing. (*She sits back in her own chair*) When you think it's completely formed. (*Pause*) Would you mind if I knit something for it?

Stella It could wear something for a week.

Caroline I'd like that. Thanks.

Stella How do you feel? About the adoption?

Caroline I don't feel anything. I don't feel a child inside me.

Stella No. (*Pause*) I could take photographs. As you get bigger. You'll be bloody beautiful.

Caroline You're different this morning.

Stella I'm wet.

Caroline Yes, but nicely. Does it happen often? Like last night?

Stella I suppose so. (*She shrugs*) I'm quite terrifying you know. (*She gets out some eye make-up remover from her handbag, dabbing off her mascara*) With men. It feels like lust, but it's loathing really. Quite cold.

Caroline Why? What's the point?

Stella Because of the way they look at you. The way they sniff about you.

Caroline Wow!

Stella They do exist, Caroline. It's not my imagination. There's something I do, have done before. If I land a really three-star macho man . . . you know, the whole image . . . never stops telling you what a great time he's going to give you. He's going to make you really cry out, you know, like drowning . . . and all this whispered or licked at you across his M.G. or yelled in your face on his Yamaha, a great gob full of, whatever, garlic or grease or fag smoke, and fucking Brut—always Brut or Prick or Stud or Come or whatever they can dream up to call that very unpleasant smell that hides that other very unpleasant smell which is the smell of them getting turned on to you—and they want to get it up through your tights in some carpark so that they don't have to cope with you afterwards, you know, because they have no feeling, nothing . . . dead eyes, dead bodies. So what I do is this. I give him . . . Mr Godsgift . . . I give him the real Penthouse cliche, right. Lick my lips, touch myself, scream a bit, play scared when he steps out of his knickers, I mean—awestruck—and I get so very excited in the first number. I always try and break things in his bedroom—preferably something expensive—because I'm so wild for it—and I give out all the words. And I can get it done in a few minutes and, well, there he is, slack-jawed, grinning, notching me up on the barrel, three-quarters asleep. So I leave him for a few minutes, then kiss him like it was love—and then I get going on him for round two. Well! Bit of a laugh, bit nervous now, Mr Godsgift, bit sheepish . . . but I'm good, OK, and he gets some response and it's going to be a great story for his pals in the morning: "You should have seen this slag—she couldn't get enough of it!" And he makes ride number two, sometimes makes ride number three, perhaps, but he's losing and he's worried and he's sore and he's fucking terrified, and the NEXT time I make certain he falls apart. I'm surprised. I'm very disappointed he can't make it. I even get angry with him. And then I get dressed and come home and stand under the shower and scrub him off me and if I could stand boiling water I'd boil myself clean to the marrow.

Caroline That's horrible.

Stella There are men doing it every day. It's my little bit to restore the balance. I mean, fuck it. If you're holding someone's hand you've only got one free to grab with.

Caroline What's the point?

Stella That's why you're so nice, Caroline. Because you're still interested in finding out. I envy you. I really do.

Caroline Is that why you do this? To harden me up?

Stella (*angrily*) That's exactly what I mean; the social worker mentality. Poor Stella—there must be a jolly good reason why she's like this.

Caroline I'm sure there is.

Stella You must tell me sometime.

Caroline It doesn't matter.

Stella No, really, I'm fascinated.

Caroline You and Kate'll get on like a house on fire.

Stella Is this your teacher friend?

Caroline Yes.

Stella We'll have to compare notes.

Caroline I didn't mean that. Kate has no notes to compare. She's gay.

Stella What. And you think I must be?

Caroline No, but you both . . . you both forgive women but you won't forgive men.

Stella Oh, come off it. I mean, what does that mean? I forgive women but not men. I can't abide most women.

Caroline It wasn't a criticism.

Stella Well, I'm not gay. That's one thing that can be said for Fran—she can't stomach all that women's movement crap. At least men laugh.

Caroline Oh, Stella! At least men have something to laugh about.

Pause

Stella What do you do? When you're down on the beach?

Caroline Nothing. Walk.

Stella Are you going today?

Caroline Probably. (*With an air of self-mockery*) D'you know why I came back here? Why I go on the beach? I thought it was going to be romantic. To walk by the sea at night, tasting the salt on my tongue. But I don't like

the cold! I spend a lot of time in cafés warming up and anyway, after all,
being pregnant isn't very spectacular, is it? Just lots of days to fill up.

Stella Can I come with you today?

Caroline (*surprised*) Yes. (*Delighted*) Yes!

Stella Right. I'll fetch the thermal underwear.

Caroline Actually, what's strange is it never feels so cold if there's two of you.

Black-out

SCENE 5

Stella and Caroline are outside. They're on bicycles, enjoying themselves

Stella What about Max?

Caroline What?

Stella If it's a boy: Max.

Caroline Max what? Maxwell or Maximillian?

Stella Max! Max-Max.

Caroline I like that. Does it get into the top three? Is it a one to watch?

Stella Well, what's there at the moment? Nathan . . . ugh!

Caroline Joshua . . .

Stella Well it's better than those two!

Caroline Max. Yes it's good! Okay—Max if it's a boy.

Stella And Stella if it's a girl. Definitely!

Caroline Oh, definitely. And we'll come to visit once a year, and have
wonderful times and eat sweets.

Stella Right, it's a deal. Wonderful times with Auntie Stella . . . only
promise—no bike rides.

Caroline Yes. Bike rides! He/she will be a cycling fanatic. He/she will have
black hair possibly, or brownish hair or blonde hair . . . black hair: all me;
brownish: me/Robin; blonde: me/John. And will laugh lots, little or not at
all . . . that's Robin lots, John little and me not at all. I'll tell you . . . it's
crucial what happens now, you know. By the time you're born, it's all
decided. This child will love the sea, bicycles and the sound of women
talking.

Stella And whale music!

Caroline It would be nice, wouldn't it?

Stella Yes, it would be nice.

Caroline Come on, slowcoach.

Stella Hang on. Caroline, I'm getting off.

Caroline No, don't stop!

Stella I'm shattered!

Caroline Oh come on, pathetic. I don't want to get off it's extraordinary.
(*Cycling off*) I don't want to get off ever . . . ever . . . ever . . . ever . . . ever.

Black-out

SCENE 6

Stella's Flat

Stella is alone. Fran enters

Fran Hello. I came as soon as I could dump Heidi. Is she upstairs?

Stella Yeah. I think she's asleep.

Fran What did the doctor say?

Stella Nothing much. He said she'd be okay. She's not going to lose it.

Fran Thank God for that.

Stella He didn't really want to know. He was very polite, but he kept saying "miss" and it stuck in his throat.

Fran Perhaps he thought she'd wanted to, that she'd ... uh ... done something to herself.

Stella Very likely. Anyway, at least she's stopped panicking.

Fran So, and what was it, she just started bleeding?

Stella Yes, apparently. But she's been down for days. I thought she was just pissed off, I mean, do you know that neither of those blokes write to her ... she's had a couple of postcards! It's pathetic. It makes me bloody weep when I see the post.

Fran What, not even her mum?

Stella Oh, she writes, and the schoolteacher friend, but, well I don't know ...

Fran That's what she wanted though, isn't it?

Stella She doesn't know what she wants. Nobody sane spends nine months lugging a spare tyre around and then gives it away to some self-righteous couple.

Fran They don't have to be self-righteous.

Stella Of course they do. You've got to be white, comfortable and self-righteous.

Fran So what do you suggest? And actually, Stella, you're wrong, actually, completely. So tell me, what do you suggest she does?

Stella OK—she's a really nice girl. She's lovely. It'll be a lovely kid. She ought to be able to keep it.

Fran She doesn't want to.

Stella How does she know?

Fran How do you?

Stella I don't, but Christ, Fran, she's got practically no choice, and that can't be right. It makes me go bloody reactionary, you know. I keep getting the urge to drag one of those men up the aisle with her. I know it's ridiculous.

Fran Well that's no use. If she's not up to keeping the child herself, marriage won't help. I mean, that's a really daft argument, it's like you get these couples who say they'll only get married if they have children, but that's rubbish because there's got to be something really tough there when a child comes along ... because it really can destroy things ... between people ... that's what happened to me, Stella, isn't it? Because, I mean, you can ignore things—but a child—if there are cracks anywhere it'll force them apart. You can be sure of that . . . I think I'll go up, anyway, see if she's okay, poor old sod.

Caroline appears in the doorway

Caroline Speak for yourself.
Stella You're supposed to be in bed.
Caroline Yes, nurse.
Stella I'm serious.
Caroline In a minute. Hello Fran.
Fran Hello love.
Caroline I'm still here. (*Sitting down*) Despite Dr Maloney and the instruments of torture. What's the matter with you two?
Stella There's nothing wrong with me.
Fran There's nothing wrong with me either. Except I've left Graeme.
Caroline You're joking.
Fran Do I mean left him? Yes, I think I do.
Stella Bloody hell!
Caroline When?
Fran Sunday. Sunday was not a good day, apparently several football teams had lost the previous afternoon. I was supposed to realize this . . . because that's why no appearance until sometime in the middle of the night. And then of course, Heidi and I are supposed to leave him alone all the next day and not talk, or you know, live much. And certainly expect no help or whatever else a man can contribute to family life. So I had a major wobbly. Oh, there was a classic—you'll love this, Stella—"Why do you think Mothercare is called Mothercare?" . . . this is a question from my husband . . . "Think about it" he said . . .
Stella I bet you did.
Fran I did not. I went to my own mother and she's caring for me!
Stella Terrific!
Fran Well, it's not permanent, I don't suppose. I'm waiting for signs of repentance. I know how many clean pairs of socks he's got left.
Stella How do you feel?
Fran All right, but my mum keeps crying. Anyway we'll sort it all out, I expect. Hey! I bought you some avocados! Any use?
Caroline What a memory!
Fran (*to Stella*) The way to Caroline's heart . . . the avocado pear.
Caroline This is absolutely true. Can I eat one now?
Stella I'll get a spoon.
Caroline Get three spoons!

Stella exits

Fran You okay?
Caroline Yes, I'm okay. He said the baby's still going strong.
Fran Stella said. That's good.

Stella enters with the spoons

Stella Three spoons.

Caroline Wonderful. These must have cost you a fortune.

Fran They did!

Stella Well bloody hell, we're celebrating!

Fran Right. I've shown Graeme the yellow card.

Caroline And I'm still pregnant.

The three girls are close and relaxed. They continue to eat happily as the Lights fade and music comes up

CURTAIN

ACT II

SCENE 1

The Seafront. Spring

Kate and D are waiting for Caroline by a children's amusement park or play ground, suggested by a climbing frame or slide, or both. D is seventeen and wearing a leather jacket decorated with political and feminist badges. She has just been spraying a poster with spray paint and has some over her hands

Kate Now you've got paint all over your hands.

D It'll come off.

Kate Christ, it's freezing. Where is she?

D I'm not cold. It's great, Kate, really exciting. It's so quiet but it's really noisy as well, isn't it?

Kate What was so offensive about that poster?

D It was sexist.

Kate How? It was for gardening tools.

D For whose garden?

Kate How should I know? Just gardens.

D Well, if it's for anyone's garden, how come you never see a woman in a gardening advert? Like on telly—who shows you how to cultivate the world's fattest potatoes? The man. And then who shows you how to peel them? His missus. That's sexist. My dad doesn't even know where our garden is. He never goes out the back door unless he's sneaking off to the pub.

Kate I see. And that will be perfectly clear to passers-by, will it?

D Yes. . . . Probably.

Kate Mummy, mummy why has that got "This is a sexist poster" written on it? Because D's Dad never goes in their garden.

D (*sulkily*) You taught me to spray posters.

Kate Did I?

D You're sorry you brought me already.

Kate I didn't bring you—I couldn't get you out of the van.

D You said I could come.

Kate Yes, I did, and here we are, getting cold. Happy?

D You're like you are in class.

Kate Really?

D Sarcastic. Unfriendly. It's because you don't want the others to know.

Kate Fine. There's nothing for them to know.

D I've told you how I feel. Are we going to sleep together?

There is a pause. Kate is flustered

    I know you want to.

Kate You don't know anything.

D No Miss, sorry Miss. Can I play on the swings, please Miss?

Kate Go to hell.

D sulks

    Oh, for God's sake. Look, I'm sorry. I can't stand long journeys. I get
ratty.

D It's not that. It's Caroline.

Kate What about her?

D You used to teach her too, didn't you?

Kate So?

D Whose baby is it?

Kate Well, it certainly isn't mine.

D No. (*Triumphantly*) She's not gay then, is she? (*She slides down the slide or
equivalent gymnastic apparatus available*) Wheee!

Kate You're very naive, D. Apart from anything else, being lesbian doesn't
stop you having children.

D Must make it hard work though. But she's not, anyway, is she?

Kate Ask her yourself.

D Is it that guy who keeps coming round to your house? Is he the father?
They're his letters, aren't they?

Kate (*shrugging*) I don't know. They're his letters.

D Why did she come down here?

Kate She was born here. It's her home.

D She should have got rid of it. I would have. The guy just gets on with his
life. Why can't she get on with hers? It's typical.

Kate Well, it's also inescapable. You can change most things, you can't
redistribute wombs.

D The day will come.

Kate I hope not.

D She could've still got rid of it.

Kate She didn't want to.

D What, just so as to give it away? Stupid.

Kate Don't act thirty. You're a very bright seventeen, you're a dim thirty.

D My English teacher told me that when someone pulls rank on you in an
argument it normally means they're losing.

Kate I never said any such thing.

D Anyway I'd hate to be thirty. I don't care if I'm dead before then.

Kate You will.

D I'm not talking about you. I'm talking about me. About my generation.
Things are moving really quickly, really fast. Seven year olds are on the pill
or they're winning Nobel prizes. Everything's speeded up. It's to do with
technology. There's no room for age now. So you've got to get everything
done, cram it in quick. I think that soon everyone will die before they're
twenty-one.

Kate Fine—we'll have to warn Caroline she's only got a day left. Who's been
selling you all this nonsense?

D Actually it's not nonsense. Lots of people know about it. It's got to
happen because there's nothing left, there's not enough energy to go round
anymore. (*She climbs to the top of the slide or frame*) I can see Caroline.
(*She waves*) She's seen us.

Kate Where? (*Scanning the landscape*) She thinks she's Sylvïa Plath, you
know. That's why she wanders around here. She's living it all out.

D Is she?

Kate Look at her. She's inside some poem—you know?—and it's very sad,
the words are, and she's wrapped them around her like sackcloth, but from
outside—to touch—it's not, it's much harder than that.

D She doesn't look sad to me. She looks bloody enormous.

Kate Where are the things for her? Have you got the bag?

D You left them in the van.

Kate Oh, good.

Caroline enters, heavily pregnant

Where've you been?

Caroline Walking. Hello.

Caroline and Kate kiss

Hello D.

D I hid in the luggage.

D looks to Kate for support, but does not get any

Caroline Fine. I hope you don't mind the floor.

D No. I can sleep anywhere.

Caroline (*smiling*) How was the journey?

D   ⎫ (*together*) ⎧ All right.
Kate ⎭   ⎩ A pain.

Caroline You must be tired.

Kate I'm frozen.

Caroline You met Stella?

Kate We said hello. How are you?

Caroline Fine. Did I tell you? I've been seeing a lot of Fran?

Kate Yes, you did.

Caroline She's fine.

Kate Are we going back?

Caroline Sorry, you're cold.

Kate Is there any food?

Caroline Oh, I don't know. Probably.

Kate We haven't eaten. I wanted to get here in daylight.

Caroline Sorry, I'm not thinking. I should have made something.

Kate We'll get a takeaway.

Caroline (*to D*) How's D?

D (*simply*) Great. It's a great place.

Caroline (*gently*) What've you got on your hands?

Kate (*laughing*) She's been defacing posters.
Caroline Ah.
Kate You can tell her about it on the way. Along with your catastrophe theory.
D No. You two go on. I'll catch up.
Kate What are you doing?
D Just going for a short walk. You two have a nice chat.

D exits

Caroline What does that mean?
Kate Search me. Oh, come on, I'm not going to run after her.
Caroline Poor Kate.
Kate (*looking after D*) Poor Kate. (*Looking at Caroline*) So . . . you look OK.
Caroline I am OK.
Kate I've missed you.
Caroline Despite D? I've missed you too.
Kate Oh yeah! I know what you miss . . . someone to wash your knickers . . . food.
Caroline Don't start.
Kate Did you get the cheque?
Caroline I will pay you back.
Kate I don't want it back.
Caroline Then don't play the martyr.
Kate Speak for yourself.
Caroline Have you seen him?
Kate Which him?
Caroline John.
Kate Yes.
Caroline And?
Kate I've seen him. Look, neither of them want to know, Caroline.
Caroline How do you know? (*She moves away*)
Kate You shouldn't have gone through with this. It's absurd.
Caroline It moves. It kicks. I can feel it.
Kate Yes. And you'll feel it afterwards too. It's conscience. And you can't have that adopted.
Caroline But I could have killed it. Is that what you're saying?
Kate No, that's not what I'm saying. (*Pause. Then angrily*) Does it make it easier, Caroline? To use those words? To justify yourself? In which case, OK. Yes. You could have killed it. Or you could keep it. But neither of those is romantic, is it?

Caroline is hurt. Stung. She moves away towards the water. Kate exhales sharply, frustratedly

(*Shouting after Caroline*) Is this what you're going to live off . . . all the pain you've stored up over the winter?
Caroline I'm happy, Kate. I could stay here for ever.
Kate Well, I'm cold, and I've got the van, and I'm driving back. Coming?

Caroline turns. A beat. She smiles. Kate smiles. Caroline returns. They embrace

Black-out

SCENE 2

Stella's Flat

Fran and D are sitting together. Stella has wet hair and is drying it with a hair dryer. Kate is apart from them, waiting for Caroline who is supposedly outside, making a telephone call to her mother

Fran Are you keen on motorbikes, then?

D No, I just like leather jackets.

Fran Oh, I see . . . I love the badges. Is that the fashion now?

D I don't know anything about fashion. Fashion stinks.

Stella Why?

D Well, for a start . . . shaving your armpits or your legs or something . . . or painting your bloody face up. It's all rubbish.

Stella You won't mind if I dry my hair?

Fran Long phone call.

Stella turns off the drier

Stella What?

Fran No. I was just saying to Kate—Caroline's been gone a long time.

Stella Oh?

Kate I don't know why her mother couldn't have come down. You'd think she might have made the effort.

Fran Well, it's quite a way, isn't it?

Kate So's Leeds. They don't want to see her, do they? Then Caroline can turn up in April with a flat stomach and they can all pretend it never happened.

Stella They might be in for a shock. I don't think she'll give it away.

Fran Nor do I.

Kate Nothing to be smug about, really, is it? Who's going to look after this baby?

Fran Lots of girls manage.

Kate Caroline can't manage herself.

Stella How do you know?

Kate I live with her. I make her bed.

Stella (*acidly*) She makes her own bed here. Perhaps she thinks you like doing it.

Kate You see, I don't think knitting matinèe jackets is caring, particularly. I think that's easy. It's like buying a child a pet.

Stella No-one's encouraging her to do anything.

Kate No? Oh, Christ, D, do you have pick your nails!

D Great party. Who died?

Fran You're right, D. It's Caroline's birthday. It won't be much of a party at this rate.

Stella It won't be much of a party anyway. Without any men.
Kate Well, that's a start.
Fran (*cheerfully*) We'll have to play some games.
Stella We'll have to get some drinks in.
D Why?
Stella Why what?
D Why do we have to get drunk, or play games?
Kate What do you suggest then?

There is a pause

D I'll go to the off-licence.
Kate No . . . I'll go. I've got the van.

D makes as if to go with her but Kate turns at the door pointedly

See you in a minute.

Black-out

SCENE 3

The Promenade. Night. The sound of gulls is heard

Caroline is alone. Kate enters, looking for her

Kate Where've you been?
Caroline Ringing my mother.
Kate For an hour? Oh Caroline.
Caroline I don't feel much like parties.
Kate No. Me neither. Let's go somewhere . . . in the van.
Caroline Where's there to go?
Kate Well, we don't have to GO anywhere. We could just get in the back and
   have our own party. I bought this in case. (*She produces a bottle of Martini*)
Caroline No thanks, Kate.
Kate Why not?
Caroline I don't want to.
Kate Why not?
Caroline And I rang John.
Kate And what did John have to say?
Caroline He played Happy Birthday on his mouth-organ.
Kate Was that instead of a card?
Caroline Oh, probably, Kate. But he's sweet.

There is a pause

   D'you know what? I keep finding myself talking to my stomach.
   Extraordinary. But it's really nice because it's not like . . . it's not the same
   as talking to yourself, is it?
Kate No, it's not the same. I want to kiss you for your birthday.

Caroline kisses Kate quickly on the cheek

Caroline Thanks . . . I think we'd better go back now.

Black-out

SCENE 4

Stella's flat

Caroline is standing in the middle of the room. A game of Charades is in progress and Caroline is holding up four fingers. Stella, Kate, Fran and D are sitting around

Stella Four words.
Kate What is it? Book, film or play?

Caroline shakes her head

It's got to be.
Fran (*who has chosen the charade*) Or a well-known phrase or saying.
Kate Typical. OK, four words.

Caroline shows her third finger, and makes the "small word" sign

Stella Third word. Small. An? At?
Kate In? With?
D To?
Stella On? Of? Off?

Caroline nods furiously

Kate Of!

Caroline shakes her head

On!

Caroline points at D

Stella To! Something something to something.

Caroline nods, raises her fourth finger and points to herself

Kate Fourth word. You?

Caroline encourages her

You? Run?

Caroline indicates "no"

Stella Girl?
D Woman? Baby? Mother?

There are "looks" all round

Caroline No.
Stella Not you. Uh . . . body? No. Uh . . . Caroline?

Caroline nods, encouraging, and does the "whole phrase" sign

Kate Whole thing. Something—Caroline? Not Caroline.

Caroline shakes her head. Makes "second word" sign

Kate OK. Second word.

Caroline shows "two syllables" sign

  Two syllables . . . first syllable . . .

Caroline points to her stomach

D Tum? Stomach? Belly? Stupid?

Caroline nods, lies down on the floor, enacts a thirty second labour, pulls out an imaginary child, slaps its bottom. "It" cries

Kate Baby.

Caroline nods. There is silence

Fran Oh come on, it's obvious.
Kate Something . . . not baby . . . to . . . you, Caroline, something.
Fran No! Do the first word, Caroline.

Caroline is upset but tries hard to look happy

Stella Pleased. Smiling. Joy. Happy!

Caroline nods

Stella Happy! Happy nearly baby to? Where does baby come into it?
Kate Birthday! Happy Birthday to . . .
Caroline Me.

A pause. Everyone is strained

Fran Right! Happy birthday to you. . . . Come on, (*singing*) "Happy Birthday" . . .

The others join in the singing

Caroline Thanks. (*At a loss*) Uh, whose turn is it?

Black-out

SCENE 5

Stella's Flat. Night

Kate and D are sleeping together in a narrow single bed. Caroline enters but seeing the situation starts to leave

Kate Wait, Caroline.
Caroline We'll wake D up.

Kate No, we won't. Put the light on.

Caroline switches a lamp on

What are you doing?

Caroline I couldn't sleep.

Kate What's the matter?

Caroline Can't get comfortable.

Kate The baby?

Caroline It's taking me over. There's no room in the bed for me. Now it's got hiccups. I'm not joking.

Kate What time is it?

Caroline I don't know. Late. Early. (*She looks at D*) She's remarkable.

Kate What? Not waking up? She doesn't sleep at night, she dies.

Caroline You're much closer, aren't you?

Kate It's a very small bed.

Caroline You know what I mean. Since I left.

Kate What do you want me to say? Look . . . I started off teaching her English, now I'm teaching her this.

Caroline God, you're patronizing.

Kate I don't think so. I'm trying to get with it. Otherwise I get hurt when lessons finish . . . you know?

Caroline It's your own doing, Kate.

Kate I'm sure it is. Well you know us gays . . . We like getting hurt. Oh, and corrupting minors, let's not forget that . . .

Caroline (*cheerfully*) Oh, shut up.

Kate Why does Stella put out that sleeping bag for us? Was she embarrassed?

Caroline I don't know.

Kate Do you talk to her?

Caroline Of course I talk to her. What do you mean?

Kate No, I mean TALK to her. Confide in her.

Caroline I suppose so. A little. Yes.

Kate Because you won't with me, will you?

There is a pause

Caroline I haven't seen you, Kate. I'm getting used to you being around again. And anyway there's D.

Kate So . . . (*She looks at D*) What's happening then? What are you going to do?

Caroline I don't know. Have the baby.

Kate And then?

Caroline And then? I don't know.

Kate Are you coming back to my house?

Caroline does not respond

You can't stay here.

Caroline Probably not, no.

Kate What have you been doing? What do you do with your days?

Caroline Walk. Think.

Kate Have you thought about me much?

Caroline Oh, Kate. I have written to you.

Kate I've thought about you, Caroline. All the time. I've been sleeping in your bed at home. . . . We could bring the child up together. I've thought about that, too. I've got enough money. We could manage.

Caroline No.

Kate I'd love her—I'd love both of you. I could look after you both, please.

Caroline I don't want to.

Kate The house is empty without you. Haven't you missed it? Haven't you missed Leeds at all?

Caroline Look, this is impossible. Yes, I've missed Leeds. For God's sake, Kate, you're in bed with D, you've got someone. I haven't missed you, Kate, if that's what you're asking me. . . . I mean, of course I have, but not in the way you want. I just don't have those feelings for you. I never have had. I'm pregnant—look!—a man did this, and I miss HIM desperately.

Kate Oh, so you *do* know who the father is.

Caroline I know who I'd like it to be. There was never anything between me and Robin. I was flattered. That he would be prepared to leave someone for me. I wasn't attracted to him. I was attracted to that.

Kate But you had sex with him.

Caroline The world doesn't stop.

Kate I wouldn't know.

Caroline No.

Kate (*bitterly*) Still, we'll be able to tell by the colour of its hair, won't we?

Caroline That's why I can't talk to you. Because you don't want to hear really, do you?

Kate Not about you with men. No, not particularly.

Caroline No. But that's it, isn't it? That's the point. Me with men—and our sex, male/female . . . and I'm not talking about some furtive thing with lights out. . . . I'm talking about wanting it. You know—just feeling like . . . well as though it were an ache. That's it . . . it IS an ache, so that it doesn't matter where you are or who's there or, it just doesn't matter you just want it. Sounds like dogs, doesn't it? But it was so good, really, with John and me. Uncomplicated. I mean I used to just touch him, outside his jeans, anywhere, under the table when we were all having coffee—really— in the house when you were due back from school. Anywhere. I got totally shameless—just for a single, uncluttered fuck, and for a long time that's all it was. I mean no technique, no theory—just grabbing. And it was terrific. Afterwards like a little boy, always, with his head on my breasts and his eyes closed. And then we started to trade that in for a whole lot of crap, like the future, and what it meant and. . . . Well, I see all these people. I mean, they can tell you about their "relationship" and what it means, and how it works, and you can just see this energy totally strangled. They're there facing each other over tables when they really want excuses to get their hands underneath the tables. I'm not talking about orgies, or rape. I'm talking about honesty, about honesty between people. . . . And I'm angry because we had that, and then we swapped it—like swapping good hard coins for a cheque book. And that's what I've missed, what I've been "thinking" about here. And maybe it's not his. If you want to know, it probably isn't. (*She laughs and sighs*) But you see, Kate, it's hopeless, isn't it? Look at us. I mean, what is D doing there! Because it's not me that's lying there beside you, it's D, and she's dreaming, and you're dreaming, and I'm dreaming and it's hopeless. I end up with Happy Birthday played down the telephone. I'm sorry . . . but sometime you had to hear that.

There is a long pause

Kate Yes, I did need to hear that Caroline. But why now? Why not a month ago? A year ago? (*She pauses*) You've always reeled me in a bit, haven't you? A look, a word, just enough to keep me there, hanging, foolish. Well, thanks. Thanks a lot.

Caroline I'm going to bed now. Goodnight.

Kate Goodnight, Caroline.

Caroline (*touching Kate*) You're my dear friend, Kate, and your letters have kept me going. Sleep tightly.

Kate You too.

Caroline goes out, turning off the light

A beat

D Kate?

Kate Yes?

D I wasn't asleep.

SCENE 6

The Beach. Late afternoon

Everyone—Caroline, Stella, Fran—is in a very loony mood. It is the late afternoon of a silly, wonderful day. They are all wearing cowboy hats and flowers and a picnic hamper is in evidence. There is a lot of fooling about and screaming. Fran has a plastic bundle—a kite

Caroline Well, I gave him a flower, and he was really sweet. Actually, yes, he gave me a fifty pence piece.

Stella What for?

Caroline For my offspring.

Stella Great. You ought to stand outside Woolies. We could make a fortune. (*In a town-crier voice*) Roll-up! Roll-up! Destitute mother . . . five kids and another on the way . . . and no room at the inn. Help fund a stable. Give generously!

Kate and D enter, D piggybacking on Kate. They, too, wear cowboy hats and flowers

Fran Come on, out of the way. Clear the runway.

There is a lot of laughter and applause as Fran displays her kite

Kate And now, this year's lucky winner of first prize at Syd's Housey-House tells us what she bought with her One Win Ticket.

Stella She didn't even know she'd won!

Fran Well, I don't know the rules.

Kate She didn't know the rules!! Do you hear that, boys and girls at home? A natural talent! So tell us, Fran, what's the prize?

Fran It's a kite.

There are "oohs" and "ahs" all round

Kate A kite! And Fran, a lovely seven-year-old housewife ...

There is much jeering at this

... from lovely Hants has won a genuine kite.

"Organ" fanfare

Worth fifteen p, she's bought it for just one twenty p go on the Bingo.

There are cheers and applause and shouts of "Speech! Speech!"

Fran I'd just like to say one thing. I've never been interviewed by a pinball wizard before!

There are whistles and yells

Kate Well now you have, girlie. (*As "Mohhamed Ali"*) I float like a butterfly, but I flips like a bee!

Stella Do you mind! We're trying to get cold here.

Fran Come on, shift your bums. We're having a test drive.

Fran and D between them charge about with the kite trailing along on the ground behind them

Fran It's off the ground ... look! Come on! Up! Up!

Sarcastic "wows" from the others

Fran There can't be any wind.

Stella You must be joking.

Kate Come on ... leave it to an expert.

Stella Rubbish!

There are chants of "Kate the Kite! Kate the Kite!"

Kate Thank you ... you'll eat your words, shitbags. I am an honorary member of the Red Arrows kite team. Out of the way, weedie, or I'll kick sand in your face.

D School bully!

Kate The very same. (*She spits on her hands, and runs away from them with the kite firmly on the ground*)

There is great applause

Actually that's not my kite. That's someone elses actually. There's mine. No, too late. It's gone into orbit. (*She collapses on the ground*) I'm dying. Argh! Minister to me. Gorge my fat carcass with cake, you hussies!

Stella and Fran rush over with cake

Stella We come, your majesty!

Stella and Fran attack Kate and stuff the cake in her mouth

Kate Get off! Argh! Help! Help! Gay-bashers!

D (*to Caroline*) How you feeling?

Caroline Fine. Exhausted. My stomach hurts from laughing. (*Looking at the cavorting*) Watch out, Fran, she bites!

Kate Yes, I do!

D It's been a really silly day.

Caroline Yes, lovely.

D Yeah, lovely. I'm really into this beach. I'm going to collect some souvenirs. D'you know—this is supposed to be where Tennyson wrote *Dream of Fair Women*?

Caroline It's a good job we weren't here when he was looking for inspiration.

Kate and Stella are now tickling Fran who makes groaning, hysterical noises

Stella It's a whale! (*She accompanies Fran with whale music*)

D (*to Caroline*) I'll be back in a minute. I'm going to go find some shells.

Kate Where you going, D?

D I'm going hunting for shells and things. Maybe have a paddle.

Kate We're just going to eat. What's the matter?

D Nothing. (*Truthfully*) I'm happy. You coming?

Kate Yeah. Sure. I'm stupid. A paddle! God! If I die, Fran, you can have my back copies of *Spare Rib*.

Fran Well hurry up—I'm ravenous.

D (*picking up the kite*) And I'm going to get this bloody thing to fly if it kills me.

Kate Don't you dare scoff all the doughnuts.

Kate and D exit

Stella Who wants some coffee?

Fran Please.

Caroline Not me. Ugh, this yoghurt's leaking! It's all over the sandwiches.

Stella What flavour?

Caroline Uh . . . muesli.

Stella Oh, that's all right then.

Fran (*examining her damaged flower*) My flower's not very well.

Stella Actually, they're really nice, aren't they?

Fran What?

Stella Those two lunatics.

Caroline Yes, they are.

Fran Kate's really different . . . you know . . . from school. Funny, isn't it? Like you expect, well I've always sort of thought that if you're . . . you know, if you don't like men, that you'd be——

Stella What are you wittering on about?

Fran Well, they're just nice, aren't they?

Stella (*laughing*) That's really deep, Fran.
Fran You know what I mean. We've had a lovely day, haven't we?

Stella starts off singing "Didn't we have a lovely time, the day we went to the seaside". Fran chimes in with whale music

Caroline (*a bit pale, piqued, lying down but speaking happily*) I'm so tired! I'm going to close my eyes and when I wake up I want it to be morning and we can start today all over again.

Fran and Stella tuck in to the picnic

Fran Do you know—I've never won anything before.
Stella Me neither.
Caroline You won Space Invaders.
Stella This is true. Was I brilliant?
Caroline Devastating.
Fran I didn't hit anything. I don't like the noise it makes when you do. (*To Caroline, indicating a coat*) Do you want this over you, love?
Caroline Please.
Stella How are things with Graeme?
Fran Oh, okay. He's taken Heidi to his sister's today. (*She bites into a doughnut*) Yes, all right, it'll never be marvellous. Um . . . this is obscene. The thing is I can't talk to him. He has made an effort . . . sort of . . . you know, after I went back, but we can't have fun . . . not like this. I never laugh. I haven't laughed like this since I was at school. Sad, isn't it?
Stella Yeah.
Fran For him too. Half the time he doesn't know why he infuriates me. Neither do I really.
Stella But you think it will last?
Fran I don't know. I know him, I'm not dim, I know what he's like . . . you know—other women and things. But then you see at the end of the day he's still my husband. He's still Heidi's dad. Does that make any sense?
Stella Yes . . . Hey! They've got it up, look!
Fran Yeah!
Stella Look at Kate! She's an absolute maniac. They're getting soaked!
Fran (*to Caroline*) Do you want something to eat?
Caroline Oh, no thanks . . . my stomach hurts. I've been laughing too much.
Stella You'd better take it easy you nut. We don't want you going into bloody labour on the beach.

Kate rushes on, kicking her wet legs at the others

Stella Get off!
Kate We got it working! Good, eh? I'm freezing! Ach, give me a doughnut before I die. Is there any coffee left? Look at D. She's like a little kid (*Yelling*) Come in number fourteen—your time is up! (*Shaking her head*) Mad as a hatter. You asleep, Caroline?
Caroline Hardly.
Kate Oh I'm so bloody wet! What am I doing? (*Lying down beside Caroline*) Well that's it. I've had it. God!

D comes on, looking mischievous, with a bucket and spade

D Mummy, mummy—I've found a contraceptive on the beach.
Kate What's a beach?
Fran O God . . . she really has! Don't be bloody revolting . . . let's have a look.

D displays the bucket

Stella Ugh, I can't stand those things. Look at it. Christ!
Fran It's a drowned semen.
Stella I thought it was supposed to be impossible underwater.
D I've decided—it's a message in a bottle.
Stella She's absolutely right. Can't read it though—it's in French!
Kate Don't show it to me, you perverts, it's probably poisonous.
Fran That's it. That's what they mean by poisonous canisters being washed up.

D teases Kate with the bucket

Kate Go away! Ugh, how gross! Girls . . . this bag has been raped.
Fran No, no, of course! It's a silly fish!

There is general laughter

Stella Silly fish! Well, that's it . . . can you imagine . . . next time you're in Boots: "Excuse me, I'd like a packet of three silly fish, please!"
Fran I don't know how it happened, Doctor, we HAVE been using silly fish.
Kate O throw it away, D. It makes me feel sick.
Caroline (*urgently*) Fran . . . I think something's happening. O God, Fran, what's happening?
Kate Caroline! What's the matter?
Stella Caroline?
Caroline Oh, my God.
Fran You'd better get the van, Kate. Stella—you ring the hospital. Tell them we're coming in. (*To Caroline*) You're going to be all right lovely. Just relax. Come on . . . remember your breathing.
Caroline What?
Fran I think you're probably going to have your baby, love. don't worry, it's all going to be fine.

Black-out

SCENE 7

A hospital side room. There is a right angle of connected grey plastic seats. One table, with a pile of magazines on it. Fran, Stella, Kate and D are there. It is late. D is asleep with her jacket over her

Fran Now I know what men feel like.

There is a pause

Stella Why do hospitals always smell the same?

There is a pause

Kate puts down a magazine, gets up and walks about

Kate This is ridiculous. What's going on?

Fran She'll be a while yet, I expect.

Kate I think they should have let one of us stay with her.

Fran Oh come on. They've been ever so good. We might have been downstairs with the dads.

Kate You're joking.

Stella Look at D.

Kate Will it be all right? I mean why is it so early?

Fran It's not that bad. A few weeks. She should be okay. They've got babies in here two months premature—perfect. It's ever such a good hospital.

Kate I didn't like that doctor.

Fran He didn't like you.

Kate Well, they're so bloody clinical. She didn't know what was going on. They should have let one of us stay with her. I mean, there's no bloody father on the scene. If there had of been they would have had him in holding a leg or whatever it is they do. I could have done that.

Stella Christ, Kate, forget it will you? There's no point. Fran's right. Things could have been a lot worse. At least they treated her like a human being. They don't always.

Fran What do you mean?

Stella Well (a) she's not married, and (b) she's giving the kid away. She's not normal, is she? I don't mean the nurses. It's the other women. They can be so bloody cruel. I've seen it. The way they say Miss. Miss.

Fran Oh I don't know. I don't think that's fair.

Stella Well . . . perhaps things have changed.

Kate Since when?

Stella Since a long time ago. (*She gets up*) Doesn't that smell get to you? That certainly hasn't changed. It's ten years since I went inside a hospital. I was pregnant. (*Very quietly*) I got pregnant when I was seventeen. Before I came down here. One fuck! I was actually in love with the bloke . . . he's married now . . . really nice guy . . .

Kate And what—did you have an abortion?

Stella No, I didn't, I was going to have the baby, that was the idea. (*Pause*) But anyway, I started to lose it. I didn't really know, but I was at home, not actually at home, round my uncle's—in the kitchen—and I was really pathetically naïve. And I was sitting in this chair, and feeling lousy, and not knowing what to do about it or what, you know, how to say anything— because, I mean, obviously my uncle didn't know what was going on. So I just sat there, and I knew I was in this pool of blood, and I just waited until he left the room, whatever he was doing, can't remember, and then just got up and rang the hospital. I mean I can't remember all the details, but they said it was hopeless, and my mother was there for a bit, and then I was in this bed, and I'd been knitting a little jacket for it, and the Nurse had come round to give me a wash, and she came back and said I shouldn't bother with knitting, but I thought bugger that, and then you know, literally minutes later, I'd sort of passed it into the bedpan. I felt like a little girl. And they got a priest and he did a kind of baptism and he gave it a name. I mean I didn't, I hadn't thought of names or anything and he said best to call it Frances, because it was impossible to say, you know, if it was a girl or a boy, so I did. Well I just said okay Frances is fine. Anyway, anyway, why am I telling you all this? . . . Oh yeah, . . . the smell, that's what reminded me. And the other women . . . smug with their rings on their fingers and their stupid husbands.

Fran That's where the matinée jacket came from for Caroline, isn't it?

Stella Yeah, I thought I might as well finish it off.

Fran You kept the wool.

Stella Oh me—I'm a right hoarder.

Kate Is it upsetting you? Being here? I could run you home, love.

Stella No, don't be daft. It's all water under the bridge. Besides, got to see it through: a bit of the old solidarity.

Kate That's it. A bit of the old solidarity.

The Nurse enters

Nurse You've got company. (*Off*) Here we are. Shall I get you a cup of coffee?

Sheelagh O'Brien, Caroline's mother, enters. She is drawn, anxious

Sheelagh Thank you. Uh, no thanks. No coffee thank you.

Nurse Okay. Right, I'll leave you to it.

Sheelagh Thanks. Hello Kate. Hello Fran.

Fran Hello. Uh, Stella, this is Caroline's mother. This is Stella.

Kate And this is D. Wake up love.

Sheelagh Oh no, don't worry . . .

D What? I was asleep.

Kate This is Caroline's mother.

There are hellos all round. Sheelagh replies with "pleased to meet you"

Sheelagh Caroline's told me how kind you've been.

Kate (*sharply*) Have you seen her?

Sheelagh They let me look in. Just for a second.

Kate Did they.

Sheelagh She wasn't really aware of what was happening, I don't think. They've given her some Pethadin.

Fran (*disappointedly*) Oh why?

Sheelagh I don't know. I should think they know what's best though, don't you? They've got one of those monitor machines on her that measures the contractions . . . and one for the baby's heartbeat. Anyway, the doctor told me they're very happy with her. . . . Do you mind if I sit down? It's quite a drive.

*Sheelagh gives the impression that she is near breaking point. The girls generate
an atmosphere that veers between sympathy and hostility*

You've all been so good to Caroline. We're very grateful.

Fran Is Mr O'Brien not with you?

Sheelagh No, he, uh, well, he's not as well as he might be. He gets very
agitated, you know, if there's any stress. I don't think he'd be much help
just now. No, but you must all be exhausted. Have you not been home or
anything?

Fran (*after a beat*) We've just been saying . . . it must be quite a novelty here
to have a pile of women pacing up and down outside the delivery room.

Sheelagh Yes, that's right. (*Compulsively putting her hand to her face*)
Goodness, I think I must be more tired than I thought. Oh, I've got some
chocolate. Would anybody like some?

Fran No, thank you.

Stella Not for me, thanks.

Sheelagh Are you sure? Go on, do have some please.

Stella Oh all right then.

Sheelagh Fran?

Fran Okay. Thanks.

Sheelagh Pass it round. Do.

Kate Thanks.

They munch the chocolate in silence. The atmosphere is very strained now

Sheelagh You must understand—I shall be fifty soon, and Caroline's my
only child, and my husband's too, and then you see, you only want what's
best, don't you? What's for the best . . .

Fran You don't have to explain to us, Mrs O'Brien.

Sheelagh No—but I don't want you to think that we don't love her, because
we do, we do love her. She's our daughter.

There is no response

She asked us not to come down, you know. . . . Did she tell you that?
Several times. But it's the same, as I said to my husband—when all's said
and done . . . it's our grandchild, isn't it?

Kate Well, don't try and persuade her to keep the baby . . . not because of
your guilt . . . not when she's so vulnerable. She's already wasted getting on
for a year. Don't ask her to waste the rest of her life.

Sheelagh And is that what you think families are? A waste?

Kate I'm not talking about families. I'm talking about a single girl with a
course to finish and no help, no father. It's not fair . . . on Caroline or the
child.

Fran Kate . . .

Kate Well, I'm angry. I'm bloody angry. You couldn't even teach Caroline
to look after herself and then you talk about families.

Sheelagh And what have you taught her? She lives in your house. Don't you
feel responsible?

Kate (*the irony not lost on her*) Oh, Christ . . . (*She sighs*) Yes, I do, actually. I
do feel pretty bad about it.

Stella I'm sorry. I don't see the point of all this.
Fran Neither do I. Blame . . . what does it matter? It won't change anything.
That baby up there in the delivery room—Caroline's baby—somewhere
around there's a couple, a woman who's been waiting for this moment.
And it's going to make them so happy. I wish people would stop talking
like the whole thing was a tragedy. No-one's died.

Kate goes over to Sheelagh and touches her

Kate I'm sorry. You start thinking of people only by their title; woman,
mother, teacher . . . I'm always shouting off about that, but I do it myself
. . . all the time.
D I've got a headache. Anyone got an aspirin?
Stella Sorry.
Fran No, sorry love.
Kate We're in a hospital, and no-one's got an aspirin.
Sheelagh Hang on, I should have some in my bag . . . somewhere . . . (*She
fishes out a box of mints*) I stopped at one of those service places on the way
down, and bought these for Caroline . . . she doesn't like mints.
Fran Well I do.
Stella (*smiling*) You're a bloody dustbin, Fran.
Fran (*smiling*) Yeah.

The Nurse comes in

Nurse I just thought you'd like to know. The head's appeared. It won't be
long now.

Black-out

SCENE 8

*The hospital ward. Caroline is in bed, surrounded by lots of flowers. Her mother
is visiting her*

Sheelagh I'd better go. Kate's waiting to come in.
Caroline Yes.
Sheelagh Did I tell you? I spoke to Daddy. He thought we might try and go
on holiday together.
Caroline He hates holidays.
Sheelagh He wants to do something for you.
Caroline Yes.
Sheelagh Well, you don't have to say yet.
Caroline Right. You'd better get off. It's a long drive.
Sheelagh It's not too bad. I surprised myself, you know, coming down.
Perhaps I'll feel less nervous now about the roads to Leeds.

Caroline nods

I wish I could stay.

Caroline There's nothing for you to do. I'm fine. Fran and Stella will supervise.
Sheelagh I used to think Fran was such a scatty girl. . . .
Caroline Oh no.
Sheelagh Oh, I realize now. Anyway, I'll go . . . (*She sighs*) . . . you know before I come in I keep thinking of all the things I want to say. . . .
Caroline There's no need, Mum.
Sheelagh I think there is, darling. . . . (*abruptly*) So—can I tell Daddy you'll think about where you'd like to go.
Caroline Did you see him, Mum?
Sheelagh Daddy?
Caroline My baby. Did you?
Sheelagh Yes.
Caroline I wanted you to.
Sheelagh Caroline—it's not too late if——
Caroline Don't . . .

The Nurse bustles by

Nurse, Nurse, how's my baby?
Nurse (*in a hurry*) Fine.
Caroline Because Sister mentioned he was a bit grizzly last night.
Nurse No, he's fine. He's bonny. All right?
Caroline Yes. Thanks. I just wondered.

The Nurse is going

(*Stopping her*) Nurse, yesterday they brought him up to me . . . you know, in the, it's not the incubator, uh . . .
Nurse Baby trolley.
Caroline Yes, the baby trolley. I just wondered whether I could, you could, whether I could see him this afternoon?
Nurse I expect that'll be all right. I'll ask Staff. OK?
Caroline Thanks. Sorry to . . .
Sheelagh (*to the Nurse*) Thanks. (*To Caroline*) That'll be nice.
Caroline Yes.
Sheelagh Everybody seems very nice. You mustn't worry about him crying. It's perfectly natural.
Caroline I know.
Sheelagh You cried all the time. Your lip always stuck out. (*She demonstrates*) Your father used to say he could sit on it. Shall I send Kate in?
Caroline Please.
Sheelagh I was thinking. It's a shame neither of your friends turned up.
Caroline Which friends?
Sheelagh I'm afraid I don't know their names . . . uh. (*She thinks, cannot remember and gives a short laugh, shaking her head*) The boys from Leeds.
Caroline (*nodding*) Oh yes. It's a shame. Whatever happens . . . we'll talk, eh?
Sheelagh Yes, that's right. Bye bye, darling.
Caroline Bye, Mum.
Sheelagh (*very quietly*) Bye.

Sheelagh exits

Kate enters

Kate Hello

A buzzer sounds

Goodbye!

Caroline I'm sorry. There's no time.

Kate Well, I'll see you next week, won't I?

Caroline I'm only going to stop a day or two, Kate. I think I ought to go home for a while.

Kate Right. . . . I rang John.

Caroline Yes. These came. (*She indicates some flowers*)

Kate He said he'd come down—if I thought it would help.

Caroline It wouldn't.

Kate That's what I said.

Caroline (*wryly*) Say it with flowers! Where's D?

Kate In the van. She says goodbye.

Caroline Well, I'll see her in Leeds won't I?

Kate I expect so.

Caroline Right. I'm glad you came. I'm glad you were here, Katie.

Kate So am I.

Caroline Have I been a fool? Is that what you think? (*Pause*) I have, haven't I?

Kate I don't know, sugar. Whatever you do, you lose. Whatever you'd done. Whatever you'd done, there's loss. It's a bugger, isn't it?

Caroline Yeah.

Kate Well hurry up and get out. You'll get soft in that bed.

Caroline My milk's come through, Kate.

Kate sighs. A pause. They embrace

Kate Every day something will happen, won't it? Today it's your milk, then there'll be birthdays and reminders and . . . for ages . . . you'll have to get tough, won't you?

They just sit there on the bed, embracing. Caroline starts beating Kate on the back

What are you doing?

Caroline Getting tough.

Kate You! (*She gets up, smiling*) See, you, shitbag.

Caroline Yeah. See you.

Staff (*off*) Come along, fathers. Out, out, out. The buzzer's gone.

Kate exits

The Staff Nurse enters

Staff Nurse says you'd like to see baby.

Caroline Please, if that's OK?

Staff You're sure you want to, now.

Caroline Yes.

Staff Well you can, but I'm afraid it can only be for a few minutes because I know that uh, Doctor Minareau and Mrs Holden have arranged for his new, for the adoptive parents to meet him today.

Caroline Ah.

Staff I think you knew that, Caroline, didn't you?

Caroline I don't know. Yes, probably, you lose track of what day it is. Oh, never mind then.

Staff I said you can see him for a few minutes now, and then later on if you want.

Caroline Lovely. Thanks. That would be lovely.

Staff So, I'll get nurse to bring him up. Now, are you still leaking a bit or is the injection taking care of it? (*She means Caroline's milk*)

Caroline It's all right I think.

Staff Good.

Staff Nurse exits

Staff (*off*) Mrs Fitzgerald, there's no need to walk like that. Goodness me! It's a baby you've had not an elephant.

Mrs Fitzgerald (*off*) It felt like an elephant.

Staff (*off*) I'm going to tell that nice husband of yours you're being an old misery guts.

We watch Caroline in bed for as long as the moment can be held whilst she faces the reality of seeing her baby

The Nurse pops her head round

Nurse Caroline, I'm sorry but they're already here.

Caroline Never mind. What a bore.

Nurse Look, I'll make sure he's brought up to you as soon as we can. Sorry. (*Pause*) Have you got enough books?

Caroline Oh yes.

Nurse It's good isn't it? So many of your friends come to see you. We were just saying. Really nice.

Caroline Right.

Nurse (*at the door*) Shout if . . .

Caroline Do they seem nice? His new mum and dad?

Nurse I don't know Caroline. I haven't met them.

Caroline But they looked nice, did they?

Nurse Uh, yes. Of course.

Caroline Can't I ask that? I'm not allowed to ask if they look nice?

Nurse I honestly have hardly seen them, but yes they seemed very nice.

Caroline I just wish people would stop treating me as if I were a martian. You know?

Nurse Uh.

Caroline Forget it. Really just forget it. Could you draw the curtains please? I'm tired. I think I'd like to sleep.

The Nurse draws the curtains and the room goes dark

SCENE 9

The Seafront

Fran, Stella and Caroline (with Heidi in her pram). Stella is carrying Caroline's haversack

Fran (*referring to Heidi*) Look at her face! And this was clean on this morning. I don't know, madam.

Stella (*laughing*) She's great.

Fran When she's asleep. (*To Heidi*) Hey, how could you manage to get choc-ice up your nose?

Stella Easy, isn't it Heidi.

Fran And she's finished it, little sod, I'm starving! (*To Heidi*) Hey, I'm starving.

Stella Christ, Fran you should be enormous.

Fran I am. I've just got a tight skin.

Stella Twit.

Fran Yeah. Holds it all in. (*To Caroline*) All right love?

Caroline Yes. I'm just having a good breathe. Souvenir.

Fran Oh, don't say that.

Stella Hey, no drama, right? If you're going to get weepy, either of you, you can piss off.

Fran Hark at tough tits.

Stella Too right. When she goes I'm going to have to get a job.

Caroline I haven't gone yet.

Stella Well, you're not staying with me. It's Spring. I'm getting out my butterfly outfit.

Caroline Wow the tourists.

Stella The idea is to frighten them off. (*Referring to Caroline's haversack*) What's in this Caroline? Bricks? You're never going to manage it yourself. Is Kate going to meet you?

Caroline Yes. Oh, listen, Fran I've left all the things, the clothes, and the books and things. Stella's got them.

Fran Lovely.

Stella And the Whale Music.

Caroline Uh, no. I kept that. I mean, I'd like to keep that if that's OK.

Fran Sure.

A woman, Veronica, walks by with a very young baby in a pram

Veronica (*to Fran*) Hello, how are you?

Fran (*uncomfortable*) OK. Just dashing.

Veronica (*to Heidi*) Isn't she a beauty? Hello fishface.

Fran She's a monster. You can have her. (*She wants to keep going*)

Veronica You're joking. (*Indicating her pram*) Yes, I'll do a swop. This one . . . no-one told him about sleep.

Fran Ha! Listen, I'll give you a call . . . or pop in or something?
Veronica Smashing.

Caroline goes up to Veronica's pram

Caroline How old is he?
Veronica He's new. He'll be three weeks tomorrow.
Caroline What do you call him?
Veronica What do we call him? Oh . . . rat . . . pig. His name is Josh.
Stella Caroline. The boat.
Caroline Right.
Veronica (*to Fran*) Bye now. Pop in.
Fran I will. Bye.

They walk on

I'm sorry. I couldn't ignore her.
Caroline Doesn't matter. Really. (*To Stella*) Josh!
Stella Urgh!
Caroline (*sighing*) Oh.

They walk on

Stella So, when shall we three meet again.
Fran Four.
Stella What? Oh, yes, four.

They reach the boat

Caroline You must come up to Leeds.
Stella Yeah.
Caroline Fat chance.
Stella I'll surprise you. Look, I'm going now. I'm a lousy waver. (*She walks away*)
Fran You'd better get on love.
Caroline Yes. I'd better . . . look, I'll . . . uh . . . you know.
Fran I know.
Caroline I want to say sorry, but I'm not sure what for.
Fran Then don't.
Stella (*walking back*) Right. Push off, I'll see you in Leeds.
Caroline (*turning sideways and putting her hand on her stomach*) It doesn't show does it?
Fran No, it doesn't show.
Caroline Not there anyway. (*She looks at them both*) Hey. . . .
Stella What?
Caroline (*thinking; shrugging*) Just hey. (*She starts to go, then turns*) See you.
Fran Yeah.

Caroline exits

The Lights fade as Stella and Fran watch her go

CURTAIN

FURNITURE AND PROPERTY LIST

Only essential furniture and properties, as required during the action of the play, are listed here

ACT I

SCENE 1

On stage: Window
Wardrobe
Bed
Chair

Personal: **Caroline:** Handbag. *In it:* money, tissues
Stella: cigarettes, matches

SCENE 2

On stage: Table. *On it:* two cups of coffee
Two chairs

Off stage: Tea, scones **(Waitress)**

Personal: **Fran:** Two carrier bags. *In one:* clothes. *In second:* records, instruction manual

SCENE 3

On stage: Two chairs
Instruction manual from previous scene
Glasses
Lucozade
Table lamp

Personal: **Stella:** cigarettes

SCENE 4

As SCENE 3 except cleared of glasses, etc.

Set: Letters, parcel containing food and chocolate

Off stage: Caroline's purse

Personal: **Stella:** handbag. *In it:* eye make-up remover, tissues

SCENE 5

Two bicycles

SCENE 6

Set as SCENE 3

Personal: **Fran:** avocados

Off stage: Spoon **(Caroline)**

ACT II

SCENE 1

Set: Playground: climbing frame or slide

Personal: **D:** spray paint, leather jacket with "badges"

SCENE 2

Set as ACT I, SCENE 3

Set: Hairdryer

SCENE 3

Off stage: Martini bottle **(Kate)**

SCENE 4

Set as ACT I, SCENE 3

SCENE 5

Set: Single bed, bedding
Sleeping bag

SCENE 6

Set: Picnic hamper. *In it:* food, including cake, sandwiches, yoghurt, flask of coffee
Coat

Personal: Everyone wears cowboy hats and flower
Fran: plastic kite

Off stage: Bucket and spade **(D)**

SCENE 7

Set: Grey plastic seats
Table. *On it:* magazines

Personal: **Sheelagh:** Handbag. *In it:* chocolate, mints

SCENE 8

Set: Hospital bed
Flowers
Curtains at window

SCENE 9

Personal: **Fran:** pram
Caroline: haversack

Off stage: Pram **(Veronica)**

LIGHTING PLOT

Various interior and exterior settings

ACT I, SCENE 1

To open: Interior lighting. Lighting outside window representing wintry seascape

Cue 1   **Caroline:** "... said I was pregnant."   (Page 4)
          Black-out

ACT I, SCENE 2

To open: Interior lighting

Cue 2   **Waitress:** "... every skirt in town ... except hers."   (Page 7)
          Black-out

ACT I, SCENE 3

To open: Interior lighting

Cue 3   **Fran:** "I'm really enjoying myself."   (Page 12)
          Black-out

ACT I, SCENE 4

To open: Morning light

Cue 4   **Caroline:** "... if there's two of you."   (Page 16)
          Black-out

ACT I, SCENE 5

To open: Exterior lighting

Cue 5   **Caroline:** "... ever ... ever ... ever ... ever."   (Page 16)
          Black-out

ACT I, SCENE 6

To open: Interior lighting

Cue 6   The girls continue eating happily   (Page 19)
          Fade to Black-out

ACT II, SCENE 1

To open: Exterior lighting

Cue 7   Kate and Caroline embrace   (Page 24)
          Black-out

ACT II, SCENE 2

To open: Interior lighting

Cue 8   **Kate:** "See you in a minute."   (Page 25)
            Black-out

ACT II, SCENE 3

To open: Night

Cue 9   **Caroline:** ". . . we'd better go back now."   (Page 26)
            Black-out

ACT II, SCENE 4

To open: Interior lighting

Cue 10   **Caroline:** "Uh, whose turn is it?"   (Page 27)
            Black-out

ACT II, SCENE 5

To open: Darkness

Cue 11   **Caroline** switches on the lamp   (Page 28)
            Snap-on lamp and covering spots

Cue 12   **Caroline** switches off lamp   (Page 30)
            Black-out

ACT II, SCENE 6

To open: Exterior lighting

Cue 13   **Fran:** ". . . it's going to be fine."   (Page 34)
            Black-out

ACT II, SCENE 7

To open: Interior lighting

Cue 14   **Nurse:** "It won't be long now."   (Page 38)
            Black-out

ACT II, SCENE 8

To open: Interior lighting

Cue 15   **Nurse** draws the curtains   (Page 42)
            Fade to Black-out

ACT II, SCENE 9

To open: Exterior lighting

Cue 16   **Caroline** exits   (Page 43)
            Fade to Black-out

EFFECTS PLOT

ACT I

No cues

ACT II

Cue 1 To open SCENE 3 (Page 25)
        Seagulls

Cue 2 **Kate:** "Hello." (Page 40)
        Buzzer

MADE AND PRINTED IN GREAT BRITAIN BY
LATIMER TREND & COMPANY LTD PLYMOUTH

MADE IN ENGLAND